Preface

THIS TEXT is a snap-shot description of a rapidly and continually evolving situation. My hope is that it may become part of the kind of conversation between concerned Christians and fellow citizens, believers and non-believers alike, which our time of crisis requires. We need all the resources at our disposal to tackle the problems facing us. It is my conviction that Christian social and theological reflection may be one such resource, of greater significance than is, perhaps, commonly appreciated.

I would like to thank Cathy Molloy, Margaret Burns, Patrick Hume, Tony O'Riordan, Frank O'Hanlon, Bill Toner, Fiona Fullam and Brian Lennon who read the text at various stages of its development and made helpful comments. This final version is, of course, my sole responsibility.

Gerry O'Hanlon SJ
Jesuit Centre for Faith and Justice
28 January 2009

First published in 2009 by

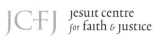

MESSENGER
PUBLICATIONS
JESUITS in IRELAND

Jesuit Centre for Faith and Justice
and Messenger Publications

ISBN 978-1-872245-64-5

Design: Messenger Publications Design Department

Printed in Ireland

THE RECESSION AND GOD

READING THE SIGNS OF THE TIMES

GERRY O'HANLON SJ

Table of Contents

'With that kind of talk
you may as well
close down the
whole country
altogether'

– angry public sector worker, in response to reported comment in January 2009 by Turlough O'Sullivan, Director General of IBEC (Irish Business and Employers Confederation), that since 10–20 per cent of private sector workers had lost their jobs, it would be right that the same percentage of public workers should lose their jobs as well.

Introduction

WE LIVE in worrying times, and the mood is ugly. In Ireland our financial and economic situation has deteriorated rapidly. Our economy is in recession, unemployment is rising sharply, there has been a severe deterioration in the state of our public finances and we are faced with unpalatable cut-backs in services. The spectre of mass emigration looms. There is a new caution about spending and planning for the future. Many of us are still somewhat bewildered and almost in denial about our plight, but increasingly one can sense a growing public and private discontent, anger, anxiety, even fear and desperation. The phenomenon of a vocal group of elderly people, protesting loudly in a Dublin city-centre church against medical card cut-backs, was an early, potent symbol of the tsunami-like shock which Ireland is experiencing.

All this is a reflection of what is happening on a larger scale world-wide. We are learning a new language: the 'credit crunch' in the USA has resulted in panic on the global financial markets, widespread economic slow-down and even recession, with civil unrest in places. As countries battle for their own economic survival, more fundamental global issues such as the UN Millennium Development Goals, including the need for environmental sustainability, are in danger of being put on the back burner.

What is going on? Often it seems that the complexity and rapidity of our changed situation are baffling even to those we imagined to be the experts – Wall Street insiders, for example, have been heard to admit that they simply did not understand quite what was going on in some of the mystifying, labyrinthine transactions which have characterised the workings of stock markets in recent years.

However, an intelligent and coordinated response is urgent and important. Apart from the many millions of ordinary lives that are being adversely affected, history teaches us that economic instability is fertile ground for political totalitarianism. The Great Depression in the late 1920s and 30s undoubtedly contributed to the rise of Hitler and Fascism. How are we to address our current situation in a way that will create the kind of economic stability capable of fostering a just peace?

Part One

Signs *of the* Times

IT WAS somewhat accidental that the group of elderly protesters in Dublin met in a church. And, in truth, even many good Christians might be puzzled that there could be a fruitful connection between their religious faith and the current financial woes of our world. What, after all, does the Blessed Trinity have to do with the likes of fiscal stimulus packages? The more classical form of this query was expressed back in the third century by Tertullian when he asked: 'What has Athens to do with Jerusalem?'

The Bishops of the Second Vatican Council (1962–5) would have been in no doubt about the answer. They boldly proclaimed that 'the joys and the hopes, the griefs and the anxieties of the people of this age, especially those who are poor or in any way afflicted, these too are the joys and hopes, the griefs and anxieties of the follower of Christ'(*Gaudium et Spes, Pastoral Constitution on the Church in the Modern World*, n. 1).

They went on to express the positive contribution that Christians and the Church can make to contemporary issues under the rubric of 'scrutinising the signs of the times' (GS, n. 4) and interpreting them in the light of the Gospel. Some important principles were articulated to guide this interpretation: in particular, respect for the legitimate autonomy of earthly affairs (including the socio-economic, political and cultural orders – GS, nn. 36, 59).

This will mean being attentive to the intelligibility and laws of particular disciplines, even while recognising that these same laws and intelligibility have their source and goal in the mystery that we call God, creator of all that is (GS, n. 36). And so, with respect to economic activity, for example, its 'fundamental purpose ... must not be profit or domination ... rather it must be service ... of the whole person ... viewed in terms of their material needs and the demands of their intellectual, moral, spiritual and religious life ... consequently, economic activity is to be carried out by its own methods and laws but within the limits of morality, so that God's plan for humankind can be realised' (GS, n. 64). There is, then, respect for the independence of economics, but this is a relative rather than an absolute independence.

This kind of tightrope way of proceeding, by means of which we respect the search for economic intelligibility and yet keep it linked to the bigger picture of human well-being and flourishing, is at the heart of the Christian contribution to our present dilemma.

A second important principle the Council asserts is that while Christians look for final solutions to the 'new earth and new heaven' that are post-historical, still 'the expectation of a new earth must not weaken but rather stimulate our concern for cultivating this one' (GS, nn. 39, 43). The Christian message will shed light on how this concern may take practical shape. However, Christians must not expect a detailed policy blueprint from this message, but rather must expect that, even among themselves, they may disagree at times on what concrete measures are to be implemented (GS, n. 43).

The Council is clearly against the kind of sacred/secular dualism which would assert either that economics on its own has all the answers, or that religion should retreat in splendid isolation to the sacristy or should preach from on high without serious dialogue with economics. Instead, under the rubric of 'reading the signs of the times', it is passionately convinced of the positive difference that Christianity can make to all our human dilemmas.

Just now it would seem that our world could do with all the help that it can get. How might we read the signs of our own times through Christian lens, in a way that might aid us to plot our way out of our current crisis with intelligence and hope?

Part Two

Biblical Inspiration:
The City upon the Hill

IN 1630, on board the flagship *Arbella*, off the coast of Massachusetts, John Winthrop addressed his fellow Puritans as follows: 'We shall be as a city upon a hill – the eyes of all people are upon us'. This biblically-inspired notion of being God's Chosen People, destined to enter the Promised Land, was shared by Winthrop's co-religionists and co-founders of what we now call the United States of America, the Separatists or Pilgrim Fathers and Mothers. It is a notion which has resonated throughout the history of the United States and finds an echo in the rhetoric of Martin Luther King and President Barack Obama.

It goes back, of course, to the belief of the Israelites, expressed through the Old or Hebrew Testament, that God had called them in a special way and had set up a Covenant or Agreement with them. This Covenant involved God's promise of fidelity to the People, and their commitment to obey God's Law (given principally to Moses in the form of the Commandments). It was an agreement which covered every aspect of life, not just some imagined 'holy', in the sense of private, domain.

The Covenant was central to the understanding of the group concerning all the major events of its history – its first exodus and sojourn in Palestine (Canaan) in the proto-historical times of Abraham (c. 2000 BC); its first Exile in Egypt and its Exodus under Moses (c. 1250); its arrival after the Desert experience in the Promised Land of Palestine under Joshua (c. 1200); its rule by Judges and then by Kings; its civil war between North (Israel) and South (Judah); its second Exile in Babylon in 598 and return in 538; its transition from the Desert Ark of the Covenant and the Ten Commandments to the establishment of Jerusalem and the

Temple as the Royal and Holy City, funded by a taxation system often experienced as oppressive.

It must not be imagined that this group narrative, part myth and part history, reflected a seamless evolution of a society in line with a neat conceptual framework shared by all. Rather it involved huge, disruptive and incomplete transitions from a nomadic to a more settled agricultural to a mixed urban–rural lifestyle; it involved skirmishes and wars with neigbouring powers like Egypt, Assyria, Babylon, Persia, the Greeks and Romans; it involved assimilation with all these groups and internal divisions about the nature of their own group. It was, in short, as complex and differentiated as the founding narrative and ongoing history of any modern nation-state, not least the founding of our own state in Ireland, emerging from that fraught and complicated, centuries-old relationship with Britain and now trying to chart its way through the troubled waters of today.

THE MEANING OF THE BIBLICAL NARRATIVE

But of course the Hebrew narrative is not simply an historical account, with all the geo-political, socio-economic and cultural factors which such an account would rightly include. It is also, and primarily, an account of faith, redolent of this nation and people's search for meaning.

Central to this account of faith is their belief that God was involved in their history. They understood themselves to have this Covenant with God, which involved a commitment on their side to monotheism and to ethical behaviour in all areas of life, in particular to social justice. Such was God's engagement with them in their day-to-day lives (as, for example, in liberating them from their lives of slavery in Egypt) that they came to recognise this God of the Covenant as also their Creator.

They were conscious of all the time reneging on their commitment: by turning in idolatry to the Baals on the High Places of Canaan, and, as the Prophets never tired of admonishing them, by mistreating the poor, the widows and the orphans. Idolatry and morality were closely connected in this understanding: worship of the fertility and nature gods of Canaan involved putting creature in place of the Creator; it involved becoming a slave of created realities like money, fame, sex, political power and sin of all kind.

Yet no amount of commandments, of Law, of wise rulers seemed able to prevent this constant turning away from God into immorality, the rejection of the liberation of the God of Exodus and the return to the Exile of sin so characteristic of the narrative. In response, there developed a hope for a Messiah, for a Messianic age in which: 'I will make a new covenant with the House of Israel and the House of Judah ... I will put my law within them, and I will write it upon their hearts; and I will be their God, and they shall be my people' (Jer, 31, 31–34).

And so Second Isaiah can say towards the end of the exile in Babylon: 'Remember not the former things, nor consider the things of old. Behold I am doing a new thing; now it springs forth, do you not perceive it?' (Is, 43, 18–19), and again, 'From this time forth I make you hear new things, hidden things which you have not known' (Is, 48, 6). The Israelites are being advised not to wallow in the past glories of Liberation/Exodus, but to hope for a new creation, a new redemption, a definitive breakthrough, which they understood to be associated with the Messiah and which would lay less stress on the externalities of Law and more on the inner heart and spirit spoken of by Jeremiah. It is in this context too that the Prophet Joel can say: 'And it shall come to pass afterward, that I will pour out my spirit on all flesh; your sons and your daughters shall prophesy, your old men shall dream dreams, and your young men shall see visions' (Joel, 2, 28–29).

It is the Christian belief that all this longing for a new Covenant, a definitive breakthrough, the pouring out of God's holy spirit are fulfilled and accomplished in the coming of Jesus Christ, his life, death and resurrection, his pouring out of his flesh and blood in the New Covenant that is given in the Eucharist and of his Spirit at Pentecost.

And so, just as the Jews constantly went back and forth in memory to events like Exodus and Exile in order to read the signs of their own times, Luke tells us that the two disciples on the road to Emmaus, downcast because of the death of Jesus and seemingly of their own hopes, were instructed by the apparent Stranger who met them on the road about the meaning of the past: 'And beginning with Moses and all the prophets he interpreted to them in all the scriptures the things concerning himself ... and their eyes were opened' (Lk, 24, 27–31). And the Eucharistic re-membering (the term is *anamnesis*, and means the making of the past present in the strongest possible sense) is that New Covenant (Lk, 22, 19; 1

Cor, 11, 24–26) which unleashes a powerful energy in the world which is like the breath or spirit with which God first created the world, the breath which infuses life into Ezekiel's dry bones, the inspiration of dreamers and visionaries, capable of overcoming all decline and sustaining all progress.

And it became clear, as had already been foreshadowed at least in God's dealing with Israel, that this breakthrough is for all people: the Christian self-understanding involves the notion of the Church as the sacrament of salvation for all – not in the sense that all must join the Church to be saved, but rather that a central function of the Church's visibility is to point to the truth that God wants all people to be saved, the Chosen People are now all God's people. The perspective has widened from a partial and limited particularity to that of an inclusive universality.

'WHERE THERE IS NO VISION, THE PEOPLE PERISH'
(Proverbs, 29, 18: King James version)

When Martin Luther King cried out 'I have a dream', when Barack Obama proclaimed repeatedly, during his campaign and after his Presidential victory, 'yes we can', they were drawing on this same biblical narrative. It is the narrative tapped into by John Winthrop for his 'city on a hill' speech, and subsequently by such diverse figures as John F. Kennedy, Ronald Reagan, Rudy Giuliani and Sarah Palin.

In our part of the world, we are not so used to this blending of the sacred and the secular: it can offend our notions of Church–State separation; it can raise fears of fundamentalism and right-wing political Evangelism. And it is true that the disparate range of politicians referred to obviously counsels against any univocal reading of the biblical narrative in its application to current situations.

Yet it would seem that trace-marks of this biblical story still have power to inspire our secular world, even when the source of this inspiration often goes unrecognised or unacknowledged. There is, as theologian James Hanvey has suggested, a kind of 'civic grace' present in the most secular of cultures.[1]

The point of the particular reading of the Bible presented above is precisely to show that this presumed separation or dualism between the so-called sacred and secular is not as obvious as it may appear at first glance. We have come, quite properly, to an understanding of the rightful autonomy of the secular. However, we must nuance this understanding to take account of the biblical claim that ultimately all is in God's hands, a claim which, again, was made so abundantly clear in President Obama's inauguration ceremony and inaugural address. We as believers do well to inquire about what practical purchase this claim may suggest.

Perhaps in what theologian Nicholas Lash calls the 'protocols against idolatry' which the Bible enjoins, and the concomitant pointers to morality and social justice, we may find a helpful tool in reading today's signs of the times? Perhaps above all in the release of that Messianic hope brought about by the Jesus event we can find the energy and vision to tackle our current situation of Exile? Perhaps we can find, like the two on the road to Emmaus, that our fear and despair may be turned once again into hope?

Part Three

Catholic Social Teaching

GERMAN CHANCELLOR Bismarck once said that you can't run a modern state relying solely on the teaching of the Sermon on the Mount. This brings us back to our earlier remark here about how on earth is one to link the language of the Blessed Trinity with that of fiscal stimulus packages.

In fact, consonant with the desire of Vatican II for a respectful dialogue with secular disciplines, there is a distinguished, sophisticated, if little known, tradition of Christian ethics which focuses precisely on this dialogue. Of particular relevance to our present discussion is the corpus of Catholic Social Teaching (CST). With its help we may adjust and refine the lens of the biblical story so as to provide a sharper reading of today's signs of the times.

At the heart of CST is an anthropology which focuses on the dignity of the human person, with concomitant rights and freedoms, and understood as having an intrinsically social nature. Two important features of this anthropology contrast with what has become almost a conventional orthodoxy of our contemporary world.

First, the human person is more than 'homo economicus' – *pace* Marx, and, ironically, his contemporary neo-liberal adversaries, the goal of all economic activity is at the service of the *humanum*, of the individual person and of humanity in general, and is not an end in itself.

Thus, in the words of Pope John Paul II, there is a priority of labour over capital, and while the economic sphere of life is important, it is so along with other areas (the personal, the cultural, the political and so on) and in service of greater overall human flourishing.

And so a warning shot is fired across the bow of the kind of 'savage capitalism'[2] which, in the phrase of novelist Tom Wolfe, the Masters of the Universe tend to practise. This then affects all of us, putting the making of money at the centre of our lives and imbuing our culture with an acquisitiveness and greed which are infectious and lead all too surely to the kind of Bonfire of the Vanities which we are now experiencing. All this, to return to the biblical story, is idolatry, and its effects lead to an Exile of individuals and peoples from the home that they are meant to find in a more balanced anthropology.

Secondly, the anthropology at the heart of CST is intrinsically social in a way that values relationships at every level – interpersonal, family, civil society, and state. It values these relationships – and the structures, systems, cultures and treaties which sustain them socially and politically – as both an end in themselves and a means of human flourishing.

In this context it should be noted that the principle of the common good, central to the application of CST to human affairs, is described as 'the sum total of social conditions which allow people, either as groups or as individuals, to reach their fulfilment more fully and more easily'.[3] I note immediately that, despite deeply-rooted fears of Liberal commentators who are suspicious of terms like the common good on the grounds that they may imply some kind of collectivist interpretation, this description holds firmly on to the notion of individual as well as group flourishing, understanding the two as intrinsically linked rather than mutually exclusive.

It should be noted that this description of the common good is both heuristic and multi-layered. By heuristic is meant that, a little like the x in algebra, it functions more as a way to discovering truth than as an already determined content: one has to engage in a search for what constitutes the common good in any given situation, a search which is guided by the description above. Similarly, there are very many different layers or horizons within which the notion of the common good operates, including the limited horizon of the socio-political and the absolute horizon of the transcendent-eschatological. Those who accept the limited good involved in the former need not necessarily – but may – also subscribe to the unlimited good of the latter. So, for example, the principle of the common good may well ground the political philosophy of a secular state, without demanding the perfection of the Gospels.

It is instructive that ethicist David Hollenbach can write, *apropos* the USA

Bishops' 1986 Letter on the Economy, that talk of the common good (in line with the dubbing of Catholic Social Teaching in general as 'our best kept secret') 'was nearly incomprehensible to most of the people the bishops sought to address'.[4] Yet such a notion of the common good may be broadly compatible with the kind of anthropology and political philosophy generated by Socrates, Plato, and Aristotle, not to mention modern systems such as civic republicanism.[5] And one notes that it is entirely consonant with the more unlimited horizon and *praxis* of the biblical Jesus, the stress by him on individual flourishing and integrity but always through love of neighbour, the value of community (the People), and all this rooted in the notion of the human as being in the image and likeness of that God who is both One and Three, in the mystery that we call Trinity.

But Modernity in general has not been happy with this notion of the intrinsically social nature of the human person. With the 'turn to the subject' in Descartes, followed by Kant's philosophical Idealism, and the more empirically based and ultimately politically oriented approaches of Hume, Locke, Mill and Hobbes, there developed in Modern times a view of the Liberal subject as an individual for whom society was often seen as at best a nuisance, at worst an obstacle.

In this context, law becomes a matter of contract, rather than based on deeper notions of the prudential application of the values of truth and justice to a pluralist society. Freedom, highly prized, is reduced to the notion of minimal constraint or coercion, as opposed to the possibility of living the good life. Politics becomes a matter of regulating that 'war of all against all' (Hobbes) or even war by other means (Foucault), in which inherently mutually conflicting forces are regulated for the benefit of the individual – it is no longer the attempt to lay the political foundations for that civilisation of love of which CST speaks, in which individual and social flourishing are co-dependent and which is inclusive of all. It may well be that elements of this managerial culture were evident in some aspects of our own laudable Social Partnership experiment over the last twenty years – one thinks, for example, of some of the excessive pay increases awarded through the benchmarking process, as well as the loss of competitiveness generally in the economy.

The extreme consequence of such a world-view was articulated (in)famously by Margaret Thatcher in her 'there is no such thing as society' remark. And it is this kind of extreme position which is at the heart of the neo-liberal economic paradigm, so influentially proposed by Friedrich von Hayek, in which there is that explicit drive to replace the state by the free market, with a confidence way beyond that of Adam Smith that the 'invisible hand' of the market is best suited to promoting individual human good by means of competition and minimal legal (and no political) regulation.[6]

Catholic Social Teaching rejects this extreme (albeit an extreme which, under the guise of a Social Darwinism and economic neo-liberalism, has become a dominant force in today's world). It does so in a way which tries to persuade more moderate Liberals that their own values can best be promoted by a more holistic approach.

And so, with liberalism, CST agrees that self-interest is not necessarily a bad thing. The notion of the common good preserves the notion of individual flourishing, as indeed, of course, does the injunction of Jesus 'to love your neighbour as yourself'. There is not, then, in CST some woolly kind of advocacy of a political altruism which, in line with Bismarck's fear about the Sermon on the Mount, would amount to a naïve and unmediated application of biblical stories to the complexities of modern situations.

The argument is rather that the true interest of individuals is best served when the interest of us all is served, when solidarity is practised, and we need to work at ways in which this situation is brought about. We need, too, to anchor our notions of freedom, law, society and politics in soil that is respectful of a notion of 'the good life' that goes beyond the external observance of rules and regulations but respects the deeper notions of justice, truth, freedom and the virtuous life.

In fact, the temptation to Social Darwinism, the survival of the fittest, the abuse of power, is always present. And because this is so, CST is emphatic that the principles of solidarity, the universal destination of goods and the preferential option for the poor must be an integral part of our understanding of the common good.

Thus, for example, it is never in the interest of individuals, no matter how wealthy they may be, that excessive inequalities exist within societies and between nations, whether these be inequalities of power or of wealth. Apart from these being an offence to that natural justice which needs to be satisfied if we are to be happy, they have the effect of increased crime, instability, even war, with concomitant negative economic consequences. Of course, as with the crisis in our environment, some may benefit in the short-term by ignoring such issues. But short-termism is short-sightedness and, as CST argues, we need to work towards a situation of sustainable economic growth, in which inequalities within and between nations are reduced and in which our environment is respected.

To get to this point will demand a more nuanced attitude to the free market: with all its advantages, it still needs appropriate political direction, and there is a role for the notion of a political economy. Otherwise, in the words of John Paul II, there is 'the risk of an "idolatry" of the market'.[7] In addition, as the Pope notes, 'there are collective and qualitative needs that cannot be satisfied by market mechanisms'[8] – one thinks of basic needs such as shelter, health-care, education, transport, welfare provision and so on, some or all of which in particular circumstances may fall outside market provision. There is indeed wisdom in the maxim that 'the market is a good servant but a very bad master'.[9]

Of particular relevance to our situation of a globalised economy, CST has been speaking for some time about the need for a better form of international, institutional, political governance of the global economy, in which all, and not just the powerful, would have appropriate representation.[10] One is reminded in this respect of the remark of John Palmer, commentator on EU affairs: 'The architecture of global governance has massive gaps in its coverage'.[11]

Secular commentators have begun to take notice of the potentially constructive contribution of CST. One notes, for example, the appreciation of Will Hutton, doyen of British writers on economics, for the daring of the Vatican in asking the kind of basic questions that politicians are refusing to ask – questions such as: how can capitalism and its market-driven dynamic be made to serve the good of everyone and not just the wealthy? Writing about a conference which he attended in the Vatican in May 2008, Hutton somewhat bemusedly comments: 'What was I doing standing in the beautiful Vatican gardens at an open-air Mass watching the green parrots swoop overhead? But there are a billion Catholics worldwide, not a trivial force for change if they can be mobilised … we stakeholders, believers in social justice and good work, make common cause with anybody we can find. And I'm delighted the Pope is one of them'.[12]

CST, in expressing the Bible story in a way that is relevant for the public affairs of today, tries to do so in a bi-lingual way that appeals to the inspiration of the Bible as a kind of deep background, but then couches its applied analysis in terms which are accessible to the ordinary canons of human reason.

As we have seen with respect to the biblical inspiration of public affairs in the United States, it is widely acknowledged that CST was extremely influential in shaping the thought of key founders of the EU and thus of the principles which inform it. In our present context it urges us to a more holistic view of the human person, which respects the importance of the economic dimension, but does not allow it to dominate. This anthropological view is integrated into a more positive approach to the notion of society and state, by means of the notion of the common good. In turn, this leads to an appreciation of the real, if limited, value of the free market; the need for appropriate political governance of the market at national and global levels in the interest of greater equality and justice, of the provision of basic needs, and of the sustainability of our environment. All this is in contrast to a liberal approach which focuses excessively on the individual, and a collectivist approach which sacrifices individual to group interest.

With this kind of sharpening of the lens afforded by the Christian story, we are in a better position to look again at our current situation and at possible ways forward. We might note, as we begin to do so, the interesting remark by Pope John Paul II, when commenting on social sin in *Reconciliatio et Paenitentia* (1984), that there is personal sin in taking 'refuge in the supposed impossibility of changing the world' (n. 16).

Part Four

A Closer Look *at our* Current Situation

We have always known that heedless self-interest was bad morals;
we know now that it is bad economics.
Franklin Delano Roosevelt, Second Inaugural Address – 20 January 1937

WHAT ARE the main salient features of our present crisis? First, putting it very simply, there has been a breakdown in trust and confidence globally in the financial and economic spheres, resulting from an at least partially dysfunctional financial sector and from the reality that too many of us in the co-called developed world (governments, banks, companies, private individuals) have been living beyond our means. The primary responsibility for all this rests with those who 'have' in our society (not, emphatically, with the poor) and disastrous consequences have followed, not just for the West, but also for the whole world and for our planet.

This 'living beyond our means' had its most dramatic and consequential manifestation in the sub-prime mortgage lending of banks in the USA. The loss of confidence and trust resulting from the defaulting on these loans led to a crisis in inter-bank lending and that tightening of credit now referred to as the 'credit crunch'. All this was exacerbated by complex and often unregulated dealings on financial markets. These involved hedge-funds, short-selling, securitisation and derivatives, including the bundling or parcelling of high-risk loans, bonds or assets into portfolios which were sold on to investors globally in a less than transparent way. All this was motivated and incentivised by short-term gains. It was driven by the desire to lend more and more in order to acquire profits and bonus payments that had little to do with the delivery of real economic performance. It has led to a massive hemorrhaging of trust and confidence.

It has seemed to the non-specialist outsider that markets have often been behaving in the smoke and mirrors manner of giant gambling casinos, with scant regard for social responsibility. And one doubts that insiders themselves were really on top of what was going on – as one commentator has put it: 'This pace of innovation and complexity simply outstripped the capacity of boards, managements and regulators to manage their institutions and the capacity of regulators to understand and limit the risks of consumers and shareholders'.[13]

This 'heedless self-interest' model of infinite-growth capitalism was replicated in varying degrees world-wide, with distinctive characteristics according to particular local situations. Thus, in Ireland,[14] we developed an excessive reliance on our construction sector, in an economy that was becoming increasingly uncompetitive (we were paying ourselves too much, 'living beyond our means'). Property prices became grossly inflated and, when this 'property bubble' burst, our banks became exposed to bad loans, so that questions were being raised not just about their liquidity and capacity to loan, but even about their very solvency. All this was against a background of strong economic growth for well over a decade, with the welcome benefits of record employment levels and a reduction in levels of consistent poverty, but with continuing high rates of relative poverty and the squandering of opportunities to enhance public services, particularly in areas like health, education, social housing and penal reform.

Opposition parties in countries like Ireland, Britain, France and so on, tend to blame their own governments for what has happened. And there may well be at least some merit to their critique. But it is clear too that our situation is of global proportions, not least because of the emergence of economic globalisation in the recent decades. The response then will have to be both local and global. What form should it take?

Ways Forward

Let me observe firstly that those of us commenting on this situation from a religious perspective may be tempted to adopt an excessively moralistic and sweeping approach. While there may be some temporary emotional release in fulminating about the idolatry of Golden Calves on the financial High Places of our world, even some gleeful *Schadenfreude* at the bewilderment of economists and politicians at what has happened, the Christian contribution calls for something more serious.

We must indeed acknowledge that our recent past was characterised by some greed, an almost giddy recklessness even (one thinks of our new wealth in Ireland). To some extent we all share responsibility for this, even if one ought to avoid any bland moral equivalence and be clear that the burden of responsibility lies particularly heavily on the shoulders of those with power, our political and economic leaders.

But the recent past was not all bad: it was, for example, wonderful that so many people in Ireland could find work, and that world-wide, particularly in India and China, there were significant reductions in the figures of those who are consistently poor.

We need then, in the language of Canadian philosopher-theologian Bernard Lonergan, to be open not just to moral but also to intellectual conversion. We need to combine our confessions of immorality with the kind of serious attention to data which will yield an understanding capable of retaining what was good in the past and building a new economic system that responds to needs in a more just and sustainable way.

REGULATION — AND?

It seems that some kind of consensus may be emerging as to how this is to be done. So, there is a new openness, at least in principle, to a less *laissez-faire*, more socially responsible economic paradigm, in which effective, properly targeted regulation and supervision of banks, financial markets and businesses becomes part of the normative culture.

There are still some ideological neo-liberal economists and commentators who may resist this notion, who believe, like Charles Krauthammer,[15] that markets should be left unregulated and that it is politics and not economics that is causing market chaos. But really, the extensive bail-out of banks in the USA and elsewhere, and the widespread introduction of Keynesian fiscal stimulus packages at the behest of financial and business interests have shattered this kind of 'small government' neo-orthodoxy unless, as some have noted ironically, this kind of 'socialism' is only for the rich, when they find themselves in need.

It will be important to get the technical details of this regulation right but also to accompany regulation with sanction. In this context I note the approach of Keith Leslie who proposes that the 'cost of failure' (to meet regulatory requirements) be at least as high as the cost of failing to meet profit expectations. So, for example, with regard to the regulatory framework of banks, 'Deeming (mortgage) foreclosures or loss of savings to be prima-facie evidence of criminal misconduct by senior management would change behaviour dramatically … and the regulatory burden could be higher for businesses that operate mis-matched bonus systems that pay out before performance is delivered'.[16]

Similarly, as noted by sociologist Michael Hornsby-Smith,[17] there needs to be a thoroughgoing reform of the bonus culture which invites financial traders to take undue risks. Instead, the reward system should be shifted from short-term profits to long-term performance.

There needs as well to be a review of the rules and funding mechanism of pension schemes. It is arguably unwise that these schemes are funded significantly by risky investment in equity markets, involving not just risk to the pension funds themselves but also putting pressure on businesses to opt for the maximisation of short-term profits at the expense of more long-term sustainability.

All this talk about rules and regulations points to something deeper. What Keith Leslie and so many others are proposing is more basic than simple regulation. In fact, some (Christopher Jamison[18]) argue that in the past, at least in the financial services industry in Britain, there has been over-regulation but no ethics, a lethal combination. With this in mind, what is required, arguably, is not more, but better regulation, in particular as applied to the so-called 'shadow banking system', involving the likes of specialist investment banks and hedge funds. However, on its own regulation can be sterile and overly-bureaucratic, it can oppose creativity and flexibility, it has a heavy hand which can lead to feelings of oppression and strategies of evasion. What we need instead is a renewed understanding of ethics which does not equate it with simple rule compliance.

Just as the threat of the 'cost of failure' led to the widespread corporate adoption of effective safety and ethical standards over the past twenty years, so too because of our present crisis we have the opportunity to motivate people, by means of a carrot and stick approach, to achieve non-economic values that are more in harmony with the common good and with the notion that the economy is at the service of the human person and not primarily and exclusively for profit. This would involve a culture in which the ethics of virtue is operative,[19] with the ethics of rules and accompanying sanctions as a kind of initial stimulus and fall-back 'long-stop'. In other words, one goes beyond a Pollyannaish, pipe-dream aspiration for virtue by appealing not just to basic human decency, but by insisting that new values and behaviour are necessary and that if they are not implemented there is a 'cost of failure'.

This notion of virtue would include the kind of prudence for which bankers were once proverbial. It would put an onus on all of us (not least for the sake of our planet and future generations) to develop a culture of moderation which avoids living beyond our means, akin to the mantra of Ghandi that: 'we need to learn to live more simply, so that others can simply live'. It would involve a commitment to a justice which cannot rest easy with the scandalous inequalities which characterise our national and, above all, global situation.

It would not be the kind of prudish virtue which dis allows the values of freedom, initiative, entrepreneurship and due profit. But it would value the kind of integrity at the heart of financial and commercial transactions that leads to that trust and confidence so necessary for an economy to flourish. We are, then, not talking about merely technical solutions and a return to 'business as usual': we are speaking about the opportunity given us by this present collapse to reframe the debate more radically.

We are talking, in particular, about the need to consider 'how realistic it is to return to the previous model of consumption-led and debt-fuelled growth'[20] – the need, in other words, to consider seriously the limits of growth, to begin the search for sustainable models of growth. This more radical approach is singularly absent from most political and financial commentary over this period: the focus on regulation alone is insufficient, and while there may be a need for fiscal stimulus packages in the short term, we also need to query the operative assumption seemingly underlying these measures that a return to the recent past is desirable.

It will be a real challenge to conceptualise and implement this more radical approach. After all, the model we have become accustomed to of consumption-led and debt-fuelled growth did produce almost full employment in many places, allowing for more inclusive participation in society. Any turn to moderation and restraint needs to take account of the value of an economy which functions sustainably for the good of all.

In this context of a search for a more radical approach it is interesting to note the observation about the role of ideas made by John Maynard Keynes, the British economist and policymaker who theorised the way out of the 1930s depression. In 1936 he wrote: 'The ideas of economists and political philosophers, both when they are right and when they are wrong, are more powerful than is commonly understood. Practical men, who believe themselves to be quite exempt from any intellectual influences, are usually the slaves of some defunct economist ... soon or late, it is ideas, not vested interests, which are dangerous for good or evil'.[21]

At its deepest this more radical approach involves a seismic cultural shift (Lonergan's notion of conversion) from the dominant individualistic, utilitarian and managerial ethos of neo-liberalism to the more inclusive ethos of the common good. But neo-liberalism was always an extreme version of the kind of liberalism world-wide that rejoices in human rights and that in countries like Britain has been to the fore in operating the welfare state. Now, with the present Sword of Damocles hanging over us due to our global economic melt-down, as well as the legally coercive measure suggested above, it may well be that many of us, Liberals and non-Liberals alike, would turn with some relief to a more humane model of economic development, respectful of our natural environment.

Roy Keane and a Humane Model of Economic Development

I remember being struck, some years ago now, when Roy Keane, still playing football then in the Premiership with Manchester United, negotiated his contract for something like 75,000 pounds sterling a week. At one level it seemed right to say: 'good on you, Roy'. At another level it seemed at best simply daft, at worst obscene.

More significantly, one could say the same, and a lot more, about the remuneration of the chief executives of banks and other businesses, often amounting to several millions a year, not to mention the profits of property developers.

Are we not uneasy with the brand of capitalism which allows, even encourages, the kind of egregious inequalities which we see evident in the contrast between the salaries of chief executives and those of the worker on the floor or in the office – not to mention the myriad other extreme inequalities of the system, from which the professions (one thinks in particular of the legal and medical) are not immune?

Even for the rampant hedonist it would seem that the sums of money involved in this make little sense: at a certain point what individual can use this kind of money, does it become simply a matter of making money for its own sake or, perhaps more likely, an envy or power-trip by means of which 'keeping up with the Joneses', 'having more possessions than the other guy' becomes the driver of economic activity?

We need to search for economic models which are less prone to such aberrations. Trade unionist David Begg[22] observes that there are at least four different socially democratic models of capitalism in Europe: the Rhineland, the Anglo-Saxon, the Mediterranean and the Nordic. He notes that the Scandinavians in particular have combined healthy growth, low unemployment, rising productivity and large export surpluses with some of the lowest levels of inequality in the world.

In a 2004 study on economic equality a group of UCD academics (John Baker, Kathleen Lynch, Sara Cantillon and Judy Walsh) note that while the Nordic countries achieve one of the most equal income distributions within the OECD by means of progressive taxation and extensive social welfare programmes, Japan has taken a different route.[23] With its brand of 'corporate welfarism' public policy has been directed at closing two gaps – 'the gap between high and low wages in different firms and industries, and the gap between economic growth and wage growth, i.e. between national economic prosperity and individual well-being'.[24] In this scenario public policy 'promotes equity in terms of wages and working conditions both within firms and between larger firms and their smaller counterparts across industries. The primary mechanism employed in relation to equity in the wage structure is the flattening of payment scales within and across firms so that the variation in pre-tax income is relatively low'.[25] Of course, the Japanese economy has had its own problems over an extended period now: it would be interesting to discover if any of these problems have to do with this 'corporate welfarism' and the drive to reduce inequality.

With the discrediting of the neo-liberal model of economic development we have an opportunity not just to tinker with the system but to reframe the debate in a way that allows notions like justice and equity to assume their proper place. Clearly in terms of technical solutions there can be no one-size-fits-all approach. Different countries start from different starting places, with histories and contexts that need to be respected. But perhaps we can get some illumination from countries and economic models that have tried seriously to address these issues. We have a new opportunity, given us by our present crisis, to think big and to go beyond management-speak in our search for that 'sustainable prosperity for all', the holy grail of political economy.[26] We need to do this in an innovative but carefully rigorous way: if one extreme is simply to tinker, another is to adopt a populist anti-market approach that simply increases poverty and unemployment, and replaces old vested interests with newer ones.

GLOBAL DIMENSION

Part of the consensus that is emerging is that any solution must involve an international, global dimension. What this means is not simply economic cooperation, but also the notion of political economy, the need to have effective global political institutions which can exercise wise stewardship over the workings of free markets. It makes sense that it is too difficult to control a global crisis with instruments that are limited to national jurisdictions, and the judgment of Cambridge academic Sir Nicholas Boyle is gaining wider acceptance: 'The world community, of which we are all part, is now paying the penalty for its failure to match economic globalisation with political globalisation'.[27]

At some level this is beginning to be remedied. The G7/8 meetings of world leaders have been recently expanded to G20, taking in most of the world's major economies, including Brazil, India, China, Saudi Arabia and South Africa. There is talk of a Bretton Woods mark 2 to refashion the global financial architecture, with increased regulatory powers proposed for the IMF and more funding for it and the World Bank.

It is heartening that these moves are afoot, and that there is some prospect of a more inclusive global economic oversight. One does not underestimate the enormous challenges that this involves, not least the effective coming together of so many countries with such different histories, interests, and structures of government and economics. The 'new thing' of Deutero-Isaiah comes to mind, the dreams and vision of Joel, the hope that now these dreams may be realised in the New Covenant with all humankind sealed by the life and death of Jesus and trumpeted forth in the 'I have a dream' and the 'yes we can' speeches of Martin Luther King and Barack Obama; and the reminder from Pope John Paul II that it is sinful 'to take refuge in the supposed impossibility of changing the world'.

We are at an early stage of this formal conversation between world leaders about what needs to be done. I would note two concerns.

First, however difficult this may be, it would seem necessary that the institutional reform to be proposed should not limit itself to the economic and financial spheres only. We have surely learned that while economics are important, they are so as a sub-set of overall human flourishing. We must not repeat the mistakes already made and think that a more efficient global economy is sufficient. We need to institutionalise the reality of a global political economy, with inclusive participation. This is particularly important to counteract the natural tendency for the strong and powerful to dominate and oppress the weak. Indeed, at both national and international levels, it should be a concern of governments that the policies they adopt to lead us out of our present crisis should do as much as possible to avoid the people who are poor having to bear the brunt of the pain – not least because it is not they who have caused this crisis.

Whether this global institutional reform can be carried out by means of the United Nations or through the creation of a different body is a matter for debate. However, it seems abundantly clear that this kind of reform is needed. It would be a considerable achievement of political innovation, evidence of a much needed 'global imagination' (Nicholas Boyle), to create democratically accountable international institutions of this kind. Kant, in his 1795 essay Perpetual Peace,[28] called for the establishment of a world civil society, a call reiterated in our day by Christian political ethicist Max Stackhouse.[29] The call for effective global political institutions is even more ambitious, but, ironically, perhaps it is at a time of crisis that this kind of innovation has the best chance of success.

Second, once again to avoid a simple return to a 'business as usual' model, we need to take serious steps to address the issues of the Millennium Development Goals, including the notion of sustainable growth in the context of the environmental crisis. Of course this presupposes a return to economic stability. But it is simply unacceptable, for example, and a scandal crying out to heaven, that, thanks to the scientific and technological gains of Modernity, we are in a position to feed the entire world, and yet so many fellow human beings continue to suffer and even die of hunger.

One way of addressing these issues is to introduce the so-called Tobin tax, as suggested by Nicholas Boyle and Paul Gillespie.[30] The late James Tobin, a Nobel Laureate in economics, proposed in the 1970s that there should be a worldwide tax on international currency transactions, to be set somewhere between 0.01 per cent and 1 per cent (Nicholas Boyle calculates that the turnover in global currency markets can run to three trillion dollars a day). His initial idea was that this tax would be a means of discouraging currency speculation. Now, however, it is being suggested that the considerable revenue this would raise could be applied to meeting the Millennium Development Goals, to funding a reformed United Nations, to setting up a stabilisation fund to guarantee the world's banking system and in general to fund the kind of sustainable development we require at global level. Is this a good idea whose time has now come?

LEADING US INTO THE FUTURE

I want to add a final note in this section about who is best placed to lead us forward out of our present crisis. At one level this is an issue of accountability, of accepting the consequences of actions. And so, without in any way advocating some vindictive witch-hunt, it is surely right for the body politic, for all of us, that mistakes are acknowledged, that we learn from them, and that just action is taken. This will involve resignations, dismissals, and even criminal prosecutions where appropriate. With regard to politicians, this can happen voluntarily (rarely the case) or, more usually, at a time of election. For leaders in the business and financial community, there are other procedures to be invoked, not least the social disapproval of culpable error.

We in Ireland, in particular, already aware of the evidence, and, in some cases, findings of so many recent Tribunals of Public Enquiry, need to question searchingly the reckless practices in public life that continue to be revealed – one thinks, for example, of the Anglo-Irish Bank debacle. These practices go way beyond the merely 'inappropriate' and, if not downright illegal, are clearly wrong. This kind of questioning is necessary in order to repair the foundations and standards of public morality so necessary to restore our national and international confidence. It must extend to the appearance at least of a kind of *laissez-faire* incompetence or even collusion in these matters between sections of the political, economic and financial establishments.

However there is another, more practical side to this issue that bears thinking about. One can be sure that most of the politicians, bankers, market traders and business leaders involved in the reckless behaviour of the recent past were not themselves, for the most part, fully aware of what was going on. They were, again in Lonergan's helpful phrase, subject to a kind of individual and group bias which permeated our culture and solidified into a 'bias of common sense'. This is said not to avoid responsibility, to assert moral equivalence between leaders and led, or to absolve of all blame. It is simply to note that it became hard to argue against the encouragement to 'party on', hard not to be affected by this cultural bias and to avoid a sneaking regard for the 'greed is good' mantra, even when, like the Israelites of old, we were uneasily aware in a part of our minds that this was idolatry, and there was even the occasional prophet who told us so. I say occasional – it now seems, like the mythical multitudes who laid claim to being in the GPO in 1916, there is a rush of experts who tell us that they got it right, 'they told us so'!

But because these leaders were subject to this bias, and because most of us take time to acknowledge our mistakes and prefer to deny and even rationalise them, they are not always the best people to engage in the kind of fresh thinking and commitment needed to lead us into the future. Already in Ireland, for example, we have seen how government politicians reject the notion that they got anything wrong; bankers have been slow to apologise for errors; and prominent property developers (Sean Dunne, Patrick Kelly, Bernard McNamara) have defended their own conduct and that of the banks. The danger in all this is that an Orwellian narrative of self-justification takes hold in the public space, on behalf of those primarily responsible for our crisis. This simply hinders the search for solutions, since these must emerge from an understanding and acknowledgement of past failures.

There is, besides, the practical difficulty that government in these times is beset with so many problems that ministers can scarcely have the time to think through a more radical approach, never mind what that might mean in policy terms. The remarks of Madeleine Bunting, with regard to the scene in Britain, have wider application: 'Is there anyone in government trying to work it out, or are they too busy trying to keep the old show on the road? Treasury ministers look boggy-eyed with exhaustion; it's hard to imagine them having the time to start thinking of the bold strategies we may need'.[31]

Of course one cannot over-generalise about this: some individuals have the power to lick their wounds and to bounce back again in a refocused way. Furthermore, we need the memory and skill of those at the centre of that *ancien régime* which contained much that was good, as well as that which we are now rejecting. The remarks of Nobel Prize winner, economist Paul Krugman are instructive in this respect, when asked about the return to the White House of Clinton-era economists in the administration of Obama: 'Well, they're smart and relatively open-minded, so they're the kind of people who can learn from their mistakes. And you do want people who know a lot about the mechanics of finance and central banking, which is why some of the people being proposed by the Left would be problematic'.[32] But we do well also to look for new faces and new ideas outside the current Establishment with, above all, a commitment to justice that is non-ideological, cognisant of the common good.

Part Five

God Matters

I HAVE noted that CST is bi-lingual, and many fair-minded but religiously agnostic commentators may well acknowledge some usefulness in the insights it offers, about our current crisis and about social reality in general, when speaking in the language of natural reason. But what about the biblical basis of this teaching, its rootedness in faith? Is this simply some kind of optional add-on?

We Christians too, all of us affected by the predominant secularism and some of us perhaps feeling on the margins of organised religion, often ask ourselves these same questions. We feel the need to understand better how God matters, and how Jesus Christ need not be confined to the private inner sanctum of our personal spiritual life.

In what follows I would like to propose a plausibility structure for the consideration that God is intimately and indispensably involved in our present situation, as a stimulus to questioning Christians and as a challenge to non-believers to think again, at least in the sense of thinking more positively about the religious contribution to difficult social issues.

GOD

Nicholas Lash[33] tells the story of the Brazilian Dominican, Frei Betto, friend of Fidel Castro, who, after a visit to England in the 1980s, noted that while everyone had warned him how secular Britain had become, he disagreed. This is not a secular, but a pagan society, he argued: it just so happens that 'we do not call the things we worship "gods"'. [34]

What Betto, somewhat provocatively, is drawing our attention to, is the innate human propensity to set our hearts on people or things in a disproportionate, absolute way that dominates our life and is, effectively, worship, but in this case the worship of idols.

Arguably this is what has happened in recent times in the West and, by imitation, globally: we have worshipped on the High Places at the Temples, not now of the Baals, but of the free market, and in the Cathedrals of irresponsible consumerism. Our faith in science and technology has become a default religion, whose empirical methods and quantifiable results have become the template, both in popular culture and in academic circles, for all reputable knowledge and truth, heedless of the truth that most of the important realities of life (relationships, happiness, justice, love) are not measurable in this kind of way. We have idolised 'getting and spending', and engaged in the cult of celebrity and fashion: a recent survey of under-10s in Britain found that Simon Colwell, the TV personality, was the 'most famous person in the world' – God and the Queen ran a close second and third![35] We have become enslaved adherents of success, and appearances, heedless of the egocentric and exploitative nature of what was going on.[36] In other words, the worship of gods – idolatry – is rife in our so-called secular society.

It is at the heart of what it is to be a Christian (or a Jew, or a Muslim) to be convinced that 'non-idolatrous worship is both possible and necessary'.[37] God, in this context, is not one larger and more powerful fact or thing belonging with other things to the furniture of this world, but rather that transcendent holy Mystery, in relation to which everything (including economics and science) has its origin and destiny (Aquinas, ST, 1a, q.1, art 7).

This means that we are radically contingent beings, vulnerable, at risk, not self-constituted. This vulnerability and risk may seem unwelcome at first, and be experienced as fear. However, in faith we believe that our contingency is rooted securely within the freely giving nature of the mystery we call God. We are creatures who are gifted into existence by God's love, and our consequent relationship of dependence is not one of servitude, but rather one of authentic freedom, with purpose and without fear.

This understanding of God as the origin and destiny of all, compatible with the notions of human freedom and truth, lays a meaningful foundation for a moral and socially just engagement with our world. Morality is impoverished when reduced to an autonomous human construction, without normative criteria. This autonomous approach, making it up, however conscientiously, as we go along, lends itself too easily to projects whose default tendency and mechanism is to favour the powerful over the weak.

We have seen how these kinds of projects have flourished historically, some of them projects with great good in them, like Liberal Modernity. They have too easily degenerated into the kind of Social Darwinism and neo-liberalism which have led to the extremes of *laissez-faire* capitalism at the heart of our present crisis. At their core is a 'thin' notion of the good, resulting in the kind of individualism which has avoided discussion of the deeper issues of the good life, and of the values of truth and justice. Many (for example, John Rawls, Jürgen Habermas and Charles Taylor) now argue that even in our pluralist societies we must find a way to engage with a 'thicker' notion of the good, as discussed by Jesuit political philosopher Patrick Riordan under the rubric of the common good.[38]

The God question, indeed, pushes us in this other direction, on a different, less egocentric trajectory in which principles like the common good and solidarity with the oppressed come to the fore. In this scenario the whole human project, with freedom and appropriate autonomy (spoken about by *Gaudium et Spes*) intact, has its basis in transcendent meaning and in the notions of the True, the Good and the Beautiful. It is not that the laws of economics, science, culture and so on are denied or ignored: rather they are set within a transcendent world of meaning in which they discover their true value as creatures and are not distorted by being mistaken for that Absolute which human hearts crave.

The God question is not, then, simply an optional add-on: the use of the God word, and this word alone, according to Karl Rahner, brings 'a person face to face with the single whole of reality' and with 'the single whole of (their) own existence'.[39] Augustine's well-know comment is apposite: 'Our hearts are restless, until they rest in You' (Confessions, Bk 1, ch1).

The Masters of Suspicion of Modernity – one thinks of Feuerbach, Nietzsche, Marx and Freud – have claimed to show that it is wishful thinking, a neurosis, an opium of the people given as a palliative to the oppressed to console them with vindication in an after-life, to suppose that God matters. I am advancing a plausibility structure for supposing that God is intimately, indispensably and benevolently involved in our world, and hence in our present crisis. I am, if you like, proposing that the hypothesis of God arguably makes more sense and gives more meaning to the data before us. The world of meaning and morality, so basic to the human project, is difficult to sustain rationally if its ultimate foundation is some theory of chance, in combination with a biological determinism. Why be moral if the meaning of life is simply a matter of chance, and may be different in the future? It is considerations like this that have led non-believers like Habermas to propose that the Liberal project in particular, if it is to be morally sustainable, may need to re-connect with its Judaeo-Christians roots and inspiration.

Now it is certainly true that the mere profession of theism, agnosticism or atheism does not of itself settle anything – 'theism can be the mask of a concealed atheism and vice versa' (Karl Rahner).[40] Indeed, we theists, by our actions, can sometimes show that we worship a God who is just another, bigger thing of this world, as we confuse God with creatures like money, sex, success, the latest theory of human self-improvement and so on. Similarly, the professed atheist who refuses to settle for the notion of reality as dull fact, but who goes on wondering and caring about our world, is in reality closer to the heart of the matter. It will always make sense, then, for all people of good will, believers and unbelievers alike, to work together for our common good.

But allowing for such ambiguities, what I am proposing to believers is the consideration that the hypothesis of God is necessary for the proper grounding of the moral life, and to believers and unbelievers alike that this notion of God can lead to constructive contributions to public debate on the way forward for our world.

JESUS CHRIST

The historical figure of Jesus Christ throws more light on the matter of God and its positive significance for our present situation.

First, the Incarnation of Jesus Christ shows us what it is to be human. In particular, it subverts our tendency to think that divinity and humanity are antithetical. In Rahner's language, humanity is not something extrinsic to God, but rather is God's mode of existence *ad extra*: 'Man is the event of a free, unmerited and forgiving, and absolute self-communication of God'.[41]

What is true of Jesus by nature, is true of us by participation: as women and men there is a spark of the divine at the heart of our humanity, we are shot through with this divinity, so it is perfectly understandable that the Greek theologians should speak of our 'divinisation'. The more divine we are, the more human we become. And thus it is also perfectly understandable that in our lives we should reach for the stars, this is the 'grandeur' of humanity, the 'yes we can' of Obama, the yearning of the world today for a way out of our crisis.

All this is, of course, the opposite of what many good people in our secular West imagine to be the notion of the good life, of human flourishing. The observations of Charles Taylor are interesting in this context.[42] Taylor judges that the issues behind secularism are perhaps not so much epistemological as cultural: we are faced not principally with a rational denial of God, but more with a moral sensibility which has persuaded itself that human flourishing is intrinsically immanent, that there is no need of a reference to the transcendent, to divinisation. The same kind of analysis is increasingly articulated by journalist John Waters in the Irish context.[43] Within this cultural framework, as the moral energy of liberalism loses force, might the Christian notion of God in Jesus Christ begin to excite imaginations again?

It might be better to say that it is Jesus Christ himself, the encounter with him, which may make the difference. Because what is involved here is not primarily a doctrine or a morality, but a relationship. In different ways in Modernity and Postmodernity we have put our faith in autonomy to make us happy; we believe that freedom of choice, freedom from coercion, is key to the good life. This is the kind of culture summed up by John Waters in terms of the myth of eternal youth, symbolised by the aura of rock 'n' roll, in which we somehow, desperately, manage to bracket out ultimate questions of meaning often associated with middle and older age by clinging to that kind of *Tír na nÓg* mentality associated with freedom.[44] But freedom of what kind? The freedom to shop, to have sex with many partners, to take away the pain of reality through addiction?

The suggestion is that in the encounter with Jesus Christ we are offered a vision of happiness which integrates an understanding of what freedom is 'for' as well as 'from': that in this encounter our deepest searchings and longings are addressed, in a way which respects, cherishes and integrates in proportion all our other desires, relationships and commitments. The suggestion indeed is that we have been looking in the wrong place for happiness – is it not foolish to believe that happiness lies in autonomy, when even in human experience our happiest moments come when we fall in love and learn to live out that love in the mature way which draws us out of egoism towards concern for others? And if, to return to Taylor's cultural diagnosis, this love is offered in a way which transcends the immanent and which responds to the deepest desires of our hearts, does it not make sense to explore the promise of such a relationship?

This is the promise offered in the encounter with Jesus Christ. To reduce it to a doctrine is to do what the Pharisees did to the Jewish notion of God, removing it from everyday currency. To reduce it to ethics is to engage in a Pelagian moralism which misses the point. Doctrine and morality are important, but they are secondary to that vital encounter with Jesus Christ who came primarily not to teach us or improve our morals but so that we might 'have life, and have it to the full' (Jn.10, 10). To reduce it to a rite of passage or to a source of consolation in troubled times is to accept that valid but impoverished notion of Christian faith which is so pervasive in our contemporary culture.

It is from that enormous love of Jesus Christ, the lodestar of our lives, the magnetic pole which draws us and shapes the whole of our life, that we come to know better (doctrine) and to serve (morals). St Augustine expressed it succinctly: 'Love, and do what you will' (7th Sermon of Commentary on First Letter of John). This is the glorious freedom of the daughters and sons of God, the sisters and brothers of the God–Man Jesus Christ, a freedom worth living and dying for. To live one's life in the company of this man is to be drawn and attracted, not driven or coerced. It is to experience joy.

And this man is also God, with a divinity that surprises, that 'empties itself', that is 'like us in all things but sin', that is approachable. In other words, but now from the side of human weakness and ordinariness, it becomes clear that humanity is compatible with divinity, that Jesus can affirm the classic lines of Terence: *'nihil humanum alienum a me puto'* – 'there is nothing that is human that is foreign to me'. There is an enormous attractiveness about this notion of humanity and the relationship with Jesus which it entails.

Because Jesus too experiences life as contingent, as depending on the one he calls Abba. And, like us, like that experience of the siren call of Satan in Modernity (Milton's 'I will not serve'), he too, in the wilderness prior to his mission, is tempted to take the short-cut to autonomy, to use naked power to bring about the blessings of God. And when, instead, he goes the way of his Father, the way of vulnerable love, yet again, like us, he finds it distressing that the cost is so high, that evil seems too strong – 'Father, take this cup from me … my God, my God, why have you forsaken me?'.

And so there is no dualism between the sacred and the secular in God's self-expression in Jesus Christ. Nor should there be in our imitation of Christ. Instead there is the enormous, ever-patient love of God drawing us from the Exile of self-alienation and injustice, through the Exodus of repentance and conversion, towards the Promised Land of the Kingdom of God, anticipations of which we experience already in our personal and communal lives.

This love of God is universal, it extends to rich and poor, to good and evil. And yet, consonant with that original 'emptying' which grounds the Incarnation, it takes the particular form of solidarity with and love of the poor, the weak, the sick, and the sinner. These were the preferred companions of Jesus, and he was criticised by the Establishment for this choice.

At stake here is a basic view of the world – riches and power tend towards idolatry and injustice, and, ironically, a certain poverty of spirit; and, in the poor and in troubled sinners, there is a certain openness to others, to God, there can be a richness of spirit. This tears up the rule-books of human logic. We are invited to consider that the notion of the good life cannot be restricted to the indispensable sphere of the economic: instead, it must also include the more important aspects of love, friendship, justice, art, poetry, nature – these are values and realities easily lost by the choking weeds of wealth and power.

But this must not lead to a spiritualising of the evils of poverty and injustice. And so even if Jesus himself disappointed some potential followers by not becoming the political Messiah widely expected, who would free the Jews from Roman rule; even if, in his famous phrase, he said 'Give to Caesar what belongs to Caesar …', thus opening the way for our modern understanding of the separation of powers between Church and State; still, this is the same Jesus who roundly turned on the free market idolatry of his day by forcibly expelling the traders and dealers at the heart of the Temple, thus reinforcing his consistent opposition throughout his active ministry to the Establishment of his day.

And so we are faced, in Jesus, with a view of God (theology) and of humanity (theological anthropology) which directs us, empowered by our relationship with God, towards a critique of abuses of power and wealth, and towards the kind of politics which addresses these issues seriously.

But we are also faced in Jesus with a claim that we are, in principle, already saved (soteriology), that his way of vulnerable love, as witnessed in the Paschal Mystery of Cross and Resurrection, has achieved a definitive victory over all evil, a victory which we are graced to appropriate.

This is what the Old Testament longed for: a definitive breakthrough from the seemingly endless cycle of God's call to justice and peace through law and commandment, the people's resistance and refusal, the punishment of Exile and then the Exodus of restoration. At last now, with Jesus, because he is that Messiah beyond expectation who is both human and divine, there has been a definitive 'yes' to this call, a breaking in principle of this wearisome cycle. This 'yes', on our behalf, has been able, in love, to endure the enormous suffering involved in absorbing in love the burden of all the terrible injustices and evil of the world which, in solidarity with victims, are gathered by the angel with his sickle and put, in that memorable phrase of the Book of Revelations, into 'a huge winepress, the winepress of God's anger' (Revelations, 14, 19).

It is within this context that someone like Martin Luther King can say that 'unearned suffering is redemptive'– in Colossians, the Pauline author expresses this in terms of rejoicing in his own sufferings because thereby he 'completes what is lacking in Christ's sufferings' (Col. 1, 24). This means that to be human is about participating in this breakthrough, this victory over evil, by sharing in the Mystery of Cross and Resurrection that shapes our lives too. It is our call to appropriate this victory freely, a project which, despite the suffering involved, can be undertaken with certain hope (1 Peter, 1, 3), without fear.

But, but – can we really, without crossing that line to myth and fairy-tale, talk so confidently about Resurrection? Cross yes, that we can imagine and have experienced too often in human history, but Resurrection – now really?! One hears in these incredulous questions the echoes of the sophisticated Athenians who mocked St Paul as he spoke to them about God before the Council of the Areopagus. All was going well until he mentioned the Resurrection: at that, the speech was over, the more polite saying 'we'd like to hear you talk about this again', with the others mocking him, bursting out laughing (Act 17, 23–34).

There is, in truth, a need for modesty, for a hermeneutic of humility and diffidence in relation to the 'how' of the Resurrection. We need to acknowledge that scriptural images in relation to the next life (the eternal banquet, the heavenly Jerusalem and so on) are just that – images, metaphors, not exact descriptions or definitions. We need to be clear that by Resurrection (whether of Jesus or of ourselves) we do not mean simple resuscitation, the continuation of life in the space and time of this world but now 'for ever'.

Rather, the Christian belief in Resurrection involves both continuity (it is still 'I' who exist) and discontinuity (I will exist in a transfigured way, as is hinted at in the appearances of the resurrected Jesus to his disciples, who both knew and did not know him), in that sphere of eternity which is best understood as the fullness and intensity of time rather than a kind of horizontal extension of everlasting time as we know it. So we can say little enough about the 'how' of Resurrection.

But we may say a little more about belief in the reality of Resurrection. Ultimately, as Karl Rahner suggests, this comes down to the question about the meaning of our existence: we are all the time striving in time and history to achieve what is beyond us and what is eternal, what alone can satisfy our desires. When we act in small and big matters in this life according to our conscience, 'whenever a free and lonely act of decision has taken place in obedience to a higher law, or in radical affirmation of love for another person' something eternal has taken place.[45] Rahner's phenomenology of the human quest for meaning, adumbrated in questions like: 'Why is any kind of radical moral cynicism impossible for any person who has discovered his real self? ... why is real moral goodness not afraid of the apparently hopeless futility of all striving?',[46] leads him to assert that death cannot be the end, that if our lives are to have meaning then that striving for the beyond which shapes them only makes sense with that promise of transcendence pre-figured in the Resurrection of Jesus Christ.

But why Resurrection as such, why not simply immortality, understood in the Greek way as the immortality of the soul, thus eliminating all the embarrassment about the survival of corporeal materiality after the radical dissolution that is death? Judaeo-Christian anthropology understands humanity as integrally matter and spirit. There is no Platonic discourse about soul being imprisoned in body, with its more modern formulation of 'the ghost in the machine'. Rather matter – and so the whole cosmos – is honoured. This is seen in Christian teachings about creation, incarnation, eucharist, marriage, all the sacraments, our social and political lives and so on: within this context of the unity of matter and spirit, the promise of Resurrection makes sense.

I have noted that we know very little about the 'how' of the Resurrection. Clearly, as outlined above, it has not to do with the resuscitation of a physical body, it has not to do with questions of cosmology, biology or physics as we understand them. Rather, just as the hypothesis of God need not clash with evolutionary theory or indeed with science in general, and just as a Christian may believe firmly and intelligently in doctrines like Creation, Incarnation, God's Providence which indicate divine transcendence within a respect for created realities, so we may firmly and intelligently believe in the hope and promise of the Resurrection, which is the ultimate guarantor and pledge of all else – of God's victory over sin and the black hole of meaninglessness: 'If there is no Resurrection of the dead, Christ himself cannot have been raised, and if Christ has not been raised then our preaching is useless and your believing it is useless … if our hope in Christ has been for this life only, we are the most unfortunate of all people' (I Cor, 15, 12–19).

It is this victory which John Donne (Holy Sonnet, n 10) hints at when he says:

One short sleep past
We wake eternally
And death shall be no more,
Death, thou shalt die.

We are invited to work that the fruits of this victory, known as the Kingdom of God, may become evident already in our world. What is involved in this process of the coming of God's Kingdom in our world?

God has come close to us in Jesus Christ: now we are the sisters and brothers of Jesus, our dignity is that of being made in the image and likeness of God. It is no wonder, then, that there is a grandeur about the human project that is God's gift to us, that we are right to use the talents given us (Mt 25, 14ff) to reach to the stars.

But there is another vector at work in human hearts and human history, the vector of sin and evil, which speaks to the misery of being human. It takes so many different shapes and forms – our personal brokenness and self-alienation, our silliness, our difficulties in fidelity to those we love, never mind to those we find it hard to get on with; inter-personal and communal strife, at all kinds of levels, including the gang-warfare in our major cities, peaking in instances such as the Gomorrah-like nightmare in a city like Naples;[47] the massive global suffering and injustice which confront us daily on our TV screens.

At the back of all this is the reality of sin in all its forms – original, personal, social. Original sin exists in that we sense some kind of struggle, a contradiction at the very heart of our being. Paul knew about this: 'I cannot understand my own behaviour. I fail to carry out the things I want to do, and I find myself doing the very things I hate' (Romans, 7, 14–15). Often enough we are indeed conscious that 'the spirit is willing, but the flesh is weak' (Mt, 26, 41–42).

This power of evil, novelist Philip Roth's The Human Stain (2000), has powerful consequences. Using Dantesque, almost apocalyptic language, Pope Benedict refers to it as developing into a 'river of evil … that has poisoned human history'.[48] The language is strong, but looking at the course of human history, at the enormous problems of our contemporary world, is there not some plausibility to this account?

At the personal level there is the reality that we are opaque to ourselves, and none of us is so self-transparent as to know quite where, in fact, our hearts are set. And so, even as we sin, we deny that we are doing so, we rationalise. In doing so we are sharing in that bias of individual, group and common sense to which Lonergan alluded: as bankers, politicians, property developers, citizens, we can scarcely believe that we did anything wrong – or that we were so stupid and uncaring. And isn't our bewildered contemporary experience as old as Adam? Think of his reply

to God's accusations: 'It was the woman you put with me; she gave me the fruit...
(Gn, 3, 12).

And Eve's reply is equally instructive: 'The serpent tempted me and I ate'
(Gn, 3, 13). We can take this as a reference to social and cosmic sin, the way that
both deep within us but also in the systems and structures of our world there is a
seemingly demonic resistance to order and good. This is the struggle against the
Principalities and Powers that Paul speaks about (Ephesians, 6, 12), that struggle
which we experience when we recognise the hydra-like existence of evil and its
atrophying into cultures and structures that seem so strong at times as to tempt
even good people into complicity. How, for example, did we as human beings live
so long with the formal toleration of slavery, of the subordination of women? How
have we been so blind to our worship of the gods of the free market? How can we
continue to be so hardened to the glaring inequalities and injustices of our world?

It is this tide of evil, this vector of sin that Jesus Christ saves us from. This
salvation is effected not by magic, not by power, but rather by that self-sacrificing,
costly, redemptive love of his which respects fully our human intelligence and
freedom. And so the struggle goes on. But now evil, personal and impersonal, is
confronted by the wonderfully attractive face of Jesus, made present by the Holy
Spirit in all its many forms of appearance in our world, healing, wooing, drawing
us away from what is evil and towards what is true, good and beautiful. The poet
Gerard Manley Hopkins perhaps conveys this omnipresence of Jesus Christ, even
where not explicitly recognised or acknowledged, in a manner more evocative than
Rahner's 'anonymous Christian':

> I say more: the just man justices;
> Keeps grace: that keeps all his goings graces;
> Acts in God's eye what in God's eye he is –
> Christ. For Christ plays in ten thousand places,
> Lovely in limbs, and lovely in eyes not his
> To the Father through the features of men's faces.
> (As Kingfishers Catch Fire)

And this is what grace is: not some kind of tablet or liquid or quantifiable 'stuff' that acts medicinally or to improve our performance, but rather a relationship of love that is beautiful and just – a love that cries out for expression not just in personal terms, but in the kind of effective solidarity that has social and political implications. These latter will involve the attempt to realise that limited common good we have spoken about earlier, with the political, social and economic structures that this entails. It will involve the kind of principled, ethical and legal behaviour that, in a fallen world, has to take account of outcomes that are less than perfect – there is a long and honourable tradition of casuistry in moral theology, which reflects on how to apply principles to concrete and even hard cases. This is a love which is often mediated through so many other relationships, through events, through nature, which allows us, through the Holy Spirit, to appropriate the victory over sin already achieved for us by Jesus Christ and to bring about his Kingdom in doing so.

Our lives, then, are shot through with the vectors of natural goodness, of sin, and of that redemptive self-sacrificing love that is called grace, the first word of all and, as we say with certain hope, the last one too. And so we are always tempted, we are always sinners, but we are also, and more significantly, being converted, being turned towards the good. This conversion will involve appropriate self-awareness and repentance: acts have consequences, there is judgment, salvation is not magic … And so, while the unconditional love and forgiveness of the Prodigal Father is the first and last word of God to all of us (including erring politicians, bankers, property developers, priests and bishops), nonetheless the Prodigal Son needs to leave the Far Country of a false autonomy, needs to learn and repent – as do all of us, in particular our leaders, *apropos* our current situation.

This conversion involves a shift from egoism to concern for others, akin to that putting on of the mind of Jesus Christ which Paul speaks about (Phil. 2, 1–8; Col 3, 12–15) and which CST expresses in its notion of the common good. And this is why Christianity, when it is lived properly, can be such a powerful force in terms of shifting a culture to a vision and values that are subversive of a complacent *status quo*. Within the vision of a civilisation of love characterised by justice it can encourage and teach values such as moderation, self-control, dialogue, respect for humanity and the earth, peace and so on – values and practices which are important if democracy is to have moral authority, and if consumption is to be responsible.[49]

This shift from egoism to concern for others is a feature of all the major religions and is another reason why the 'cold war' between secularists and people of religion needs to come to an end: all people of good will need to be in solidarity if good is to triumph. Indeed this seems to be the thinking also of the Institute for Public Policy Research, the UK's leading progressive think-tank, which in a recent, pioneering study of religious faith and the public realm in Britain, advises that 'British progressives in particular have good reason to take seriously the political scientist Robert Putnam's contention that religions remains one of the most reliable and impressive sources of social capital'.[50] The Institute authors also quote the remark of the Chief Rabbi Jonathan Sachs that 'Religion is an agent of social change, the most powerful there is', and note that he proposes that religions in Britain come together to create a 'covenant of the common good'.[51]

The hardest of us – think of Raskolnikov in Dostoyevsky's *Crime and Punishment*, his evil heart melting, like snow under the sun, before the gaze of Sonia's love – may change when eye to eye with the beauty of love. The Holy Spirit is at work in our world bringing the look of love from God, from Jesus Christ to us all. We matter that much to God, who freely 'loves us to bits', loves us in fact 'to death'. Grace, as Bonhoeffer said, is costly. And God is this intimately bound up with all creation but, in particular, with each one of us and with the destiny of the human race.

If Jesus Christ is the image, and in this sense, the sacrament of God, then the Church, the sphere of the Spirit, may be considered as the sacrament of Jesus Christ. As such, the Church is not primarily self-referent, but is rather a sign to the world of God's presence. The Church then points to the Kingdom, which is much larger than the Church itself. And at the heart of the Church's own sacramental system is the Eucharist, in which we participate in that sacrifice of redemptive love of the New Covenant, are even invited to be co-sufferers with Christ in offering this sacrifice; and we share too in the meal which inaugurated this sacrifice and at which the ritual washing of feet was to be a sign of that sacrament of love and service of neighbour which is the essence of Christian living.

With this kind of notion of Eucharist, recalling the 'subversive memory' of Jesus (Metz), it is easy to see why Eamon Duffy, referring to Timothy Radcliffe's study of the Eucharist,[52] can suggest that 'to go to church, therefore, is not a comforting routine for the secure and incurious, but a place of expectation, challenge and growth: the appropriate headgear is not posh hats, but crash helmets'. In the same vein Daniel O'Leary says 'we would strap ourselves to our seats' if we understand the full impact of what was happening around us when we attend Mass.[53]

Of course it also true that often we don't live out of this understanding and that, moreover, the Church itself is made up of sinners as well as saints. This is reflected in its deficiencies of acts, omissions and systems, often, sadly, of a quite scandalous and shocking nature. But nonetheless, while itself living out the mystery that the wheat and tares will be together till the end, the Church has to remain faithful to her mission of being a beacon of hope to our world, by daring to take out the light of Jesus Christ from under the bushel, despite her own failings. Mostly, of course, this mission is carried out without fuss or drama in the ordinary lives of Christian women and men, being a leaven in our world, the salt that gives flavour. Occasionally, there are dramatic events which highlight at world level the force for good and wonder which that more usually hidden holiness may evoke only in smaller, more anonymous circles: perhaps the funeral of Pope John Paul II, and the respectful media attention which it evoked, was one such occasion.

The Christian attitude to the world is one of hope rather than optimism. There can be a lot of sentimental 'ooing and aahing' at Christmas time over the baby Jesus wrapped in his swaddling clothes in a crib. But, to paraphrase Irish author and playwright Aidan Matthews, this is a sad drama which begins badly and will end worse. The Scriptures themselves give the lead on this: the birth is actually in a situation of poverty and vulnerability, and early on Mary is told that 'a sword will pierce your heart'.

This is all of a piece with that almost incredible sense of risk and contingency with which the human Jesus Christ (and hence God's own self) puts his fate in our hands. Think first how dependent his very existence was on the 'yes' (fiat) of Mary: the scene is presented in Luke (1, 26–38) in a dramatic way, Mary is disturbed, she questions, this is no computer game with a pre-scripted automatic outcome. Mary had to freely say yes: what if she had said no? And if this latter is unimaginable, think how Jesus himself hoped that the Jews would accept his Good News, but they didn't, there was massive resistance and it did end badly, on a cross.

And now it is our chance, and are we, like blustering Peter, so confident that we will never betray the Lord, never say 'no'? Remember what is asked is enormous: personal conversion, to love enemies, to discover the jewels of humanity in those outside my own comfort zone, to fight for a better world not in some abstract way but now, in our concrete situation of global crisis.

This is why we speak of hope rather than optimism. Hope is there precisely when things look bleak, not rosy. Surprisingly indeed it can be found in the bleakest of places (visitors to heart-creakingly difficult situations in parts of Africa, for example, are often struck by the vibrancy of hope in apparently hopeless conditions). Hope is for the long haul, it grounds human resilience. But how are we to understand the grounds for this hope itself, a hope that we are told is certain?

HOPE

The myth of inevitable progress, which fuelled Modernity, has had its Postmodern expression in Fukuyama's End of History thesis when it seemed, with the fall of the Berlin Wall, that liberal democracy and free market capitalism were somehow the final and ideal expression of human government. There have been some Christian expressions of this notion of inner-worldly progress (one thinks of Irenaeus, Joachim of Fiore, Teilhard de Chardin), but the more classic Christian theology of history is more nuanced.

In this classic view history is seen as a going out *(exitus)* and return *(reditus)* to God in which the vectors of progress, decline and redemptive love constantly interact with our intelligence and freedom in a way that is far from linear, but more like a spiral of troughs, plateaus and peaks. Within this spiral it is far easier to predict progress at the level of the scientific and technical, far more difficult to be so sure about moral progress. We have gone from the printing presses and wars of Reformation times to the computers and even more savage wars of our own times.

Christian hope takes realistic account of the power of evil at all levels and is aware of the apocalyptic scenarios which this can engender. Its form is eschatological: that's to say, it believes that God's kingdom will come fully at the end, post-history, but that already we can glimpse partial, imperfect but real anticipations of it.

The hope for universal salvation at the end, including the vindication of all those who have died without any inner-worldly justice, is expressed biblically in such terms as the New Jerusalem, 'the new heavens and new earth' (2 Peter, 3, 8–14), the heavenly banquet and so on. Theologically it is expressed daringly in von Balthasar's image of the Cross of Christ at the far side of hell, still saving. The message is clear: despite the awful weight of evil, the terrible harm we do one another, the apparently ineluctable force of vested interests and inhumane structures, still the wonderfully creative, ever compassionate and faithful love of God will find a way to achieve the divine goal of universal salvation with complete respect for our human freedom.

But what about the 'already', the this-worldly presence of the Kingdom, all the human hopes for a better world now and in our historical future? The reality and experience of evil cautions us against any facile optimism. We know too that there is no claim biblically or in CST that we have a blueprint for socio-political and economic world development. We realise that the Sermon on the Mount, as Bismarck noted, is not 'fit for purpose' as an unmediated instrument of political government. We can see the sense in the separation of spheres between Church and State, even if we might rightly cavil at the relegation of the Church to the private sphere alone.

But, with all these caveats, there are no grounds, in the name of 'Christian realism', to put a limit to the answer that God can give to our daily prayer of 'thy Kingdom come'. With intelligence, good will, commitment, and all in consonance with God's Providential plan and dream for our world, we can celebrate the partial but so wonderful successes of the end of apartheid in South Africa, the movement for civil rights in the USA, the peace settlement in Northern Ireland and the many other instances of communal and personal grace which we experience right through our lives. There exists an Ariadne's thread out of the Old Testament labyrinth of seemingly eternal temptation, sin and conversion, out of the enormous struggle with evil in our world – and perhaps we can already see the emerging evidence that God can write straight on the crooked lines of our contemporary fascination with the idols of wealth and autonomy.

It is worth recalling, again, that the achievements cited above are but partial and flawed, and that God's part in them is not to be understood as some kind of magical, direct intervention. God does not work in our world like some Sky Wizard, 'zapping' enemies left, right and centre, or like a Cosmic Engineer, ever on hand to overcome obstacles and repair damage. Rather God's providential working in the world is accomplished much more along the analogy of the way a lover is affected by his or her Beloved: I am drawn towards the truth and goodness of my Beloved, this changes me. There is causality at work here, but not of a blunt efficient kind: this is more the causality of knowing and loving, of relationship. We – and analogously all creation – are drawn and lured towards the true and the good that find their absolute personification in God alone. This truth and goodness are written, as it were, into the DNA of our humanity, and implicitly or explicitly we are invited to respond accordingly. Our response will involve both knowing (the search for truth) and loving (the empowerment to do what we know is required). And thus, throughout history, in response to this patient wooing by God, imperfect realisations of the common good are achieved, not least through that self-sacrifice of redemptive love which undoes the surd of evil created by us.

We do well to remember that God, through Jesus Christ and in the power of the Spirit, is the primary actor in all this, even while our whole-hearted response and effort are required. And, as in all personal relationships, our freedom is always respected. These considerations ought to make us less anxious, less fanatical in our search for a better world – its achievement does not depend only or even mainly on our efforts, indispensable though they are. And it is consoling and energising to realise that all our desires and dreams for a better world are part of our prayer to God, part indeed of God's prayer in us, that groaning which accompanies the birth pangs and first-fruits of creation in the process of liberation and is a sign of the Spirit's working within us (Romans, 8, 21–23).

But it does also involve our cooperative action – the intellectual conversion that shows itself in attention to data, in steady and yet inventive reflection on problems; the moral conversion that moves us from exclusive self-interest to a commitment to the common good; the religious conversion, God's love flooding our hearts, that, above all, casts out fear and mobilises intelligent action.

And within this cooperative project two other particular aspects deserve mention. First, the way God works in our world, the way the Kingdom comes, has a counter-intuitive dimension to it that we need to be aware of. St Francis of Assisi, according to Chesterton, after his conversion stood on his head to indicate that he now saw the world in an upside-down fashion. Jesus gave first place to the poor, he left the ninety-nine sheep to save the lost one, he was born in a cave outside a town (no room at the inn), and, to paraphrase Aidan Matthews again, he died in a public execution as a condemned criminal in a rubbish dump outside the city, far away from our leafy suburbs. Any proposed managerial solutions to our present crisis that do not take on board this disturbing solidarity with and indeed preference for the poor and oppressed is simply missing the point and lacking credibility.

Second, there is clearly a significant role to be played by leaders of all kinds (political, business, religious) in our search for a better world. With regard to politicians in particular the notion of public service is crucial, very much in line with the example given by Jesus at what we call his Last Supper.

With the appearance of a leader of the stature of Barack Obama in the United States many people throughout the world have grown in hope, even according him an almost messianic devotion. We need of course to be careful here. Jesus as the unique God–Man is the only one who can perform the decisive act which can bring about our salvation. Nonetheless, with all due respect for the inevitable obstacles and even failures which characterise the efforts of even great women and men, we do well to acknowledge that all leaders in some way participate in the Lordship of Jesus Christ, and to rejoice in the hope which gifted and graced leadership can inspire in us.

I note, finally, that the structure of our hope is Trinitarian. The God who matters, origin and end of all, is revealed as our Father; Jesus Christ is the Son, our brother; the Holy Spirit is the bond of love uniting this diversity of relationship into that profound unity which permits us to speak of the Mystery of the One God. We are called into this life of God, by the initiative of the Father, through the decisive *kenosis* or emptying of the Son in taking on humanity to the point of Cross and Resurrection, and in the power of the Spirit. This is the Trinity of St Ignatius of Loyola, presented to our imaginations as seated on the Divine Throne, looking down on our troubled world and saying 'let us work the redemption of the human race' (*Spiritual Exercises*, 106).

This Trinity of unity-in-diversity allows for the presence of the Spirit and seeds of the Word that is the Son to be present in the many world religions other than Christianity. The approach here has been from a Christian perspective. This perspective is increasingly aware and accepting of the presence of God working through all religions. The theological understanding of this truth is perhaps in an early stage of development, but already it has become apparent that the dialogue of theological ideas will learn from the other dialogues of life, action and religious experience which point the Christian towards the need to engage with devotees of other faiths in our search for a better world.

This is also a Trinity of *kenosis*, of self-emptying, of solidarity. And this *kenosis* for the Christian will involve too the movement away from another comfort zone, that of engaging solely with fellow-religionists. Instead, we are called to engage and work not just with those of other religions, but also with agnostics and atheists, within that widespread culture of secularism in which there are often so many examples of that 'civic grace' which James Hanvey speaks about. Even with that bi-lingual approach of CST, in which secular language finds a home, this can be a difficult task because of the in-built resistance in the dominant liberal culture to the notion that people of faith might have a constructive and substantial contribution to make to the issues of the day. We need to avoid wallowing in a kind of victimhood in this matter (the media as anti-Christ!), and instead take our courage in our hands, be a bit more daring, and believe that in the end truth has its own powers of persuasion (and indeed, that we, as Vatican II articulated so well, have a lot to learn about the truth from our secular co-citizens).

Modernity prized the value of freedom greatly, and understood it predominantly in terms of a strong individualism with weak social ties. Postmodernity seems to allow more scope for the group or community, but with a weak, de-centred notion of the subject. Taken together they have been a fertile breeding ground for the recent dominance and excesses of the neo-liberal brand of capitalism. God, it might be agreed, is the ultimately free, autonomous Subject. And yet God is revealed to us as the Trinitarian Mystery, a symbol of interdependence. We, who are made in God's image and likeness, do well to take notice.

Conclusion

It was an ideology, not an act of God, that made this crisis possible.
Paul Krugman, December 2008

But in the words of Scripture (I Cor 13, 11) the time has come to set aside childish things ... to choose our better history ... the God-given promise that all are equal, all are free, and all deserve a chance to pursue their full measure of happiness.
President Barack Obama, Inaugural Address, 20 January 2009

WE ARE experiencing what seems like another Babylonian Captivity in the form of our current global crisis. Bewilderment, fear and anger are common; we are even tempted to lose hope.

We are in a human situation not unlike that of the two disciples on the road to Emmaus. There the Stranger who joined them on the way helped them to reflect on the meaning of the past so as to open up a future full of hope.

While detailed technical solutions have been beyond the scope of this essay, it seems that there are fairly clear and agreed broad lines along which our future should go, if we can learn from our past. These involve a more socially responsible economic paradigm, with greater regulation at national but also global level.

However, it has also been proposed here that this consensus does not go far enough. There needs to be a real effort at cultural change, so that we begin to live the kind of sustainable life compatible with moderate growth expectations, respect for the environment, and an effective solidarity which rejects the gross inequalities within and between nations. We need to place the common good at the heart of our concern and to search for the new kind of economic and political models which may embody this concern. At a time of crisis we have an opportunity for this new kind of thinking, vision and values. High-flown rhetoric, a return to the heady 1960s and the notion that the 'future is socialist', will not be adequate. We need intelligent problem-solving, but within a wider conceptual framework than a simple return to 'business as usual' model.

I have suggested that CST gives some pointers as to how this might be achieved. In this context, we need the Church itself to appropriate this teaching more fully and engage with our world accordingly. In this era of Postmodernity in the West in general, but perhaps in particular because of our Irish experience of secularisation and clerical scandal, the Church can seem quite timid, focused excessively on its own identity or seemingly exclusively on socially conservative issues. We seem to be somewhat complacent about the great issues of our day, complicit rather than subversive, lacking, as an institution, that passionate engagement which characterised our founder in his own day.

Obviously, we need to work to change this, even if it will take time. Of more immediate prospect is the formation of clusters, movements, coalitions, campaigns, networks, even at some stage perhaps political parties, from people with a shared concern for our future. Some of these people will be inspired by religious faith, others not. Not all will agree on specific policy issues. But we can realistically hope for this kind of alliance at the level of civil society, within the kind of respectful pluralism which allows for different (religious and non-religious) sources of inspiration, but which shares the same basic concern for a more adequate expression of our common good.

And, of course, there is no simple connection between the Mystery of the Blessed Trinity and fiscal stimulus packages. But I hope to have shown that 'scrutinising the Signs of the Times' leads to the conclusion that religion is properly and intimately concerned with this crisis of our day, in all its aspects. That while God is active – indeed is the principal actor – in our world, this is not to be conceived along the 'act of God' lines which insurance companies use to invoke the occurrence of seemingly inexplicable natural events, but rather along the lines of that transcendent origin, sustainer and end of all creation, completely respectful of human freedom, wooing us towards that relationship with the divine which people of faith acknowledge as the only ultimate satisfaction of human desire, and towards that multi-layered expression of our common good sought by all people of good will. And that our religious faith can help us to be less afraid, give us hope, offer insight and harness energy for the next, so-important, steps of our journey, to be taken together with all fellow-citizens and fellow-human beings.

Throughout this journey we are held by the safe and loving embrace of our God, and in this gift we may trust absolutely. It is a gift presented to us above all in the person of Jesus Christ, made accessible now by his Spirit. This is precisely the point where prayer and worship, redolent of gratitude and joy, combine with an intelligent commitment to a politics that will engage in that difficult and sometimes even ferocious search and struggle for what is good. It is why French poet Charles Péguy could say that 'everything begins in mysticism and ends in politics'.

References

[1] James Hanvey SJ, 'Deus Caritas Est: The God who is Love in the World' in *The Institute Series, 5: Deo Caritas Est* (pp. 9–40), London: Heythrop Institute for Religion, Ethics and Public Life, p. 20.

[2] The phrase attributed to Pope John Paul II – cf Clifford Longley, *The Tablet*, 23 August 2008, pp. 10–11.

[3] Pontifical Council for Justice and Peace, *Compendium of the Social Doctrine of the Catholic Church*, Dublin: Veritas, 2005, n. 164.

[4] Quoted in John A. Coleman SJ (ed.), *Christian Political Ethics*, Princeton and Oxford: Princeton University Press, 2008, p. 170.

[5] cf Iseult Honohan, *Civic Republicanism*, London and New York: Routledge, 2002, ch. 5.

[6] cf Angus Sibley, 'The Cult of Capitalism', *Doctrine and Life*, 58, November 2008, pp. 11–20.

[7] Sibley, *op. cit.*, p 15.

[8] *Ibid.*

[9] Jesuit Centre for Faith and Justice, 'Justice in Recession: Statement on the Current Economic Situation', *Working Notes*, 59, November 2008, p. 7.

[10] Pontifical Council for Justice and Peace, *op cit*, nn. 371–72; 440–42.

[11] John Palmer, 'European Integration: A Vital Step on the Road to a New World Order', in Jesuit Centre for Faith and Justice, *The Future of Europe: Uniting Vision, Values and Citizens* (pp. 130–39), Dublin: Veritas, 2006, p. 136.

[2] *The Observer*, Sunday, 1 June 2008.

[13] Keith Leslie, 'What Really Caused the Crash of 2008', *The Tablet*, 4 October 2008, p. 4.

[14] cf Oliver Maloney, 'Secularism and the Current Economic Crisis', *The Furrow*, 60, January 2009, for a perceptive commentary on the Irish version of this self-interest model, and its connections with secularism; cf also The Irish Commission for Justice and Social Affairs (ICJSA), *In the Wake of the Celtic Tiger: Poverty in Contemporary Ireland*, Dublin: Veritas, 2009, for a reflection on the many faces of poverty in Ireland, in the context of the notion of the common good.

[15] *The Irish Times*, Tuesday, 2 December 2008.

[16] Keith Leslie, *op. cit.*, *The Tablet*, 4 October 2008, p. 4.

[17] Michael Hornsby-Smith, 'First, Protect the Weak, *The Tablet,* 22 November 2008, pp. 13–14.

[18] Christopher Jamison, 'Might of Metaphysics', *The Tablet,* 15 November 2008, pp. 9–10.

[19] Seamus Murphy SJ, 'The Many Ways of Justice', *Studies in the Spirituality of Jesuits,* 26/2, March 1994, and 'Virtue Ethics and Christian Moral Reflection', *Milltown Studies,* 55, 2005, pp. 82–112.

[20] Paul Gillespie, *The Irish Times,* Saturday, 11 January 2009.

[21] Quoted by Paul Gillespie, *The Irish Times,* Saturday, 11 January 2009.

[22] David Begg, 'The Future of the European Union: Economic Growth, Social Cohesion and Sustainability', in Jesuit Centre for Faith and Justice, *The Future of Europe: Uniting Vision, Values and Citizens,* Dublin: Veritas, 2006, pp. 73–82; 'Solidarity and Freedom: Defending the Rights and Dignity of Work in a Global Economy', in Eoin G. Cassidy (ed.), *The Common Good in an Unequal World,* Dublin: Veritas, 2007, pp. 129–46.

[23] John Baker, Kathleen Lynch, Sara Cantillon and Judy Walsh, *Equality,* London: Palgrave Macmillan, 2004.

[24] *Ibid.,* p. 90.

[25] *Ibid.,* pp. 90–91.

[26] Clifford Longley, 'An Acceptable Face for Capitalism', *The Tablet,* 23 August 2008, p. 10.

[27] Nicholas Boyle, 'A Tax to Save the World', *The Tablet,* 25 October 2008, p. 6.

[28] Quoted by Paul Gillespie, *The Irish Times,* Saturday, 13 December 2008.

[29] Max Stackhouse, 'Christianity and the Prospects for a New Global Order', in John A. Coleman SJ (ed.), *Christian Political Ethics, op. cit.,* pp. 155–69.

[30] cf Nicholas Boyle, *op. cit.,* p. 7; Paul Gillespie, *The Irish Times,* Saturday, 8 November 2008.

[31] *The Guardian,* 6 October 2008.

[32] In an online interview with Andrew Leonard – http://www.salon.com/tech/htww/feature/2008/12/08/paul_krugman/index.html

[33] For what follows, cf. Nicholas Lash, *Theology for Pilgrims,* London: Darton, Longman and Todd, 2008, especially ch. 2, 'The Impossibility of Atheism', pp. 19–35.

[34] *Ibid.,* p. 22.

[35] cf http://news.sky.com/skynews/Home/UK-News/Simon-Cowell-More-Famous-Than-God-Or-The-Queen-Survey-Of-British-Kids-Under-10/Article/200812315180581?f=rss

[36] M. Dolors Oller i Sala, *Building a Sense of Community*, Barcelona: Cristianisme i Jucticia, 131, October 2008, pp. 24 ff.

[37] Nicholas Lash, *op. cit.*, p. 22.

[38] Patrick Riordan SJ, *A Politics of the Common Good,* Dublin: Institute of Public Administration, 1996; see also, *A Grammar of the Common Good: How to Make Sense of Globalization,* London: Continuum, 2008 (Continuum Studies in Religion and Political Culture).

[39] Nicholas Lash, *op. cit.*, p. 24.

[40] In Nicholas Lash, *op. cit.*, p. 34.

[41] *Ibid.*, p. 26.

[42] cf M. P. Gallagher, 'Charles Taylor's Critique of "Secularisation"', *Studies*, 97, Winter 2008, pp. 433–44.

[43] See, for example, John Waters, *The Irish Times,* Friday, 9 January 2009.

[44] John Waters, 'The Sabotage of Hope', *The Furrow,* December 2008, pp. 651–61.

[45] Karl Rahner, *Foundations of Christian Faith,* New York: Seabury Press, 1978, p. 439.

[46] Karl Rahner, *op. cit.*, p 438; also *Encyclopedia of Theology,* London: Burns and Oates, 1975, p. 1440.

[47] Presented on screen by director Matteo Garrone, after the book by Roberto Savino.

[48] *The Tablet*, 6 December 2008, p. 34.

[49] M. Dolors Oller i Sala, *op. cit.*, pp. 24–28.

[50] Zaki Cooper and Guy Lodge (eds.), *Faith in the Nation: Religion, Identity and the Public Realm in Britain Today,* London: Institute for Public Policy Research, 2008, p. 67.

[51] *Ibid.*, p. 36.

[52] Eamon Duffy, 'Make Sure to Wear a Crash Helmet', Review of Timothy Radcliffe's *Why Go to Church? The Drama of the Eucharist, The Tablet,* 17 December 2008, p. 40.

[53] Daniel O'Leary, 'Shock Waves of Bethlehem', *The Tablet,* 20/27December, 2008, p. 4.